Copyright © 2018 Jennifer Sharpe

All rights reserved. No part of this publication may transmitted in any form or by any means, including electronic or mechanical means, without the prior written permission of the publisher. Reviewers have permission to use brief passages and images from the book for review purposes only.

ISBN-13: 978-1719225410

ISBN-10: 1719225419

Graphics: @Charlotte Braddock 2015
http://www.teacherspayteachers.com/Store/Charlottes-Clips-4150

Fonts: @Kaitliynn Albani
https://www.teacherspayteachers.com/Product/KA-Fonts-Complete-Font-Bundle-Growing-Bundle-2828325

Scripture texts in this work are taken from the New American Bible, revised edition © 2010, 1991, 1986, 1970 Confraternity of Christian Doctrine, Washington, D.C. and are used by permission of the copyright owner. All Rights Reserved. No part of the New American Bible may be reproduced in any form without permission in writing from the copyright owner.

Every reasonable effort has been made to determine copyright holders of excerpted materials, fonts, and graphics and to secure permissions as needed. If any copyrighted materials have been inadvertently used without proper credit being given, please contact Jennifer Sharpe in writing so that future editions may be corrected.

Book Design by Jennifer Sharpe

Published by Jennifer Sharpe

Contact:
jennifersharpe.author@gmail.com
fb.me/jennifersharpe.author

My First INTERACTIVE mass book
for Catholic Kids

This Book Belongs To:

Keep in Touch!

Like my book?

Leave an Amazon review! It only takes a moment, and it really helps!

I love hearing your feedback!

Have a question? Want to review my book on your blog or website? Feel free to contact me by email any time!

Email:
jennifersharpe.author@gmail.com

New books are coming out all the time! Follow me on Facebook for giveaways, discounts, book walk-through videos, and updates on my work:

Facebook Author Page:
fb.me/jennifersharpe.author

Amazon Author Page:
amazon.com/author/jennifersharpe

Help your older children learn to love the Mass too with my other book:

The Mass Book for Catholic Children, a guided Mass journal geared toward ages 7 to 12. Available on Amazon.com and other online retailers.

A Note For Parents

Please see the back pages of this book for ideas on how to use the book with your child.

My First Interactive Mass Book for Catholic Kids has one goal in mind – to help your child grow closer to Jesus in the Eucharist. To do this, this book seeks to engage the child at his or her own level in all that is happening during each Mass. The book follows the order of the Mass, and includes all the main prayers, interspersed with carefully planned interactive pages to ensure your child is getting the most out of the Mass. From a visual schedule of the Mass, to a "spot the Mass items" activity, to a page for choosing the correct liturgical color for the priest to wear, this book has what it takes to help cultivate a sense of belonging and participation for your child at Mass.

There are two ways you can choose to use this book. The first way is to follow the instructions at the back of this book to make removable pieces that your child can use to interact with the book at each Mass. The other way is to simply use the book as-is. Both ways work equally well. If you would like to use the book as-is, you may skip to #2 below. Otherwise, be sure to read the whole page.

Before You Begin:

①. If you would like to use the removable components, INTRODUCE THE BOOK TO YOUR CHILD AND PREPARE THE INTERACTIVE PAGES AHEAD OF TIME. Read through the book, cut out the pages at the back, and laminate them or cover them with clear contact paper (my favorite way). Then have your child find the correct pages for each item and attach them. You will need to purchase something to adhere the loose pieces to the book, and I recommend using **Scotch Restickable Mini-Tabs for Mounting** or **Scotch Create Reusable Mini Squares** for this purpose. There are full instructions in the back of this book to guide you through the steps of making your book interactive. *Do not use removable components with children under 3, as they may pose a choking hazard.

②. BRING THE BOOK TO MASS EVERY WEEK. Your child may need some extra help the first few times, but in no time at all they will be using the book independently and following along with all the different parts of the Mass all on their own. You should introduce the book to them ahead of time, so that they are familiar with the flow of the book, and how to complete each activity.

All Catholic parents desire for their children to learn to love the Mass, especially Jesus in the Eucharist. Your child needs your gentle guidance from the start. May this book help you to help your children truly enjoy and look forward to participating in Mass every week.

I Pray Before Mass

I'm glad I'm at Mass today, Jesus.

Help me use my ears to listen to you during the readings.

Help me use my eyes to see that you are really there in the Host.

Help me quiet my body so that I can pay attention to all that you want to show me today.

Most of all, help me to know how much you love me!

Amen.

The Order of the Mass

	1. Procession		5. Gifts
	2. First and Second Readings		6. Consecration
	3. Gospel Reading		7. Communion
	4. Homily		8. Final Blessing

I Can Bless Myself With Holy Water

Dip your finger in the holy water and make the Sign of the Cross each time you come to Mass to remind yourself of your baptism. You can also pretend to dip your finger into the holy water font on this page, and then touch each number to make the Sign of the Cross!

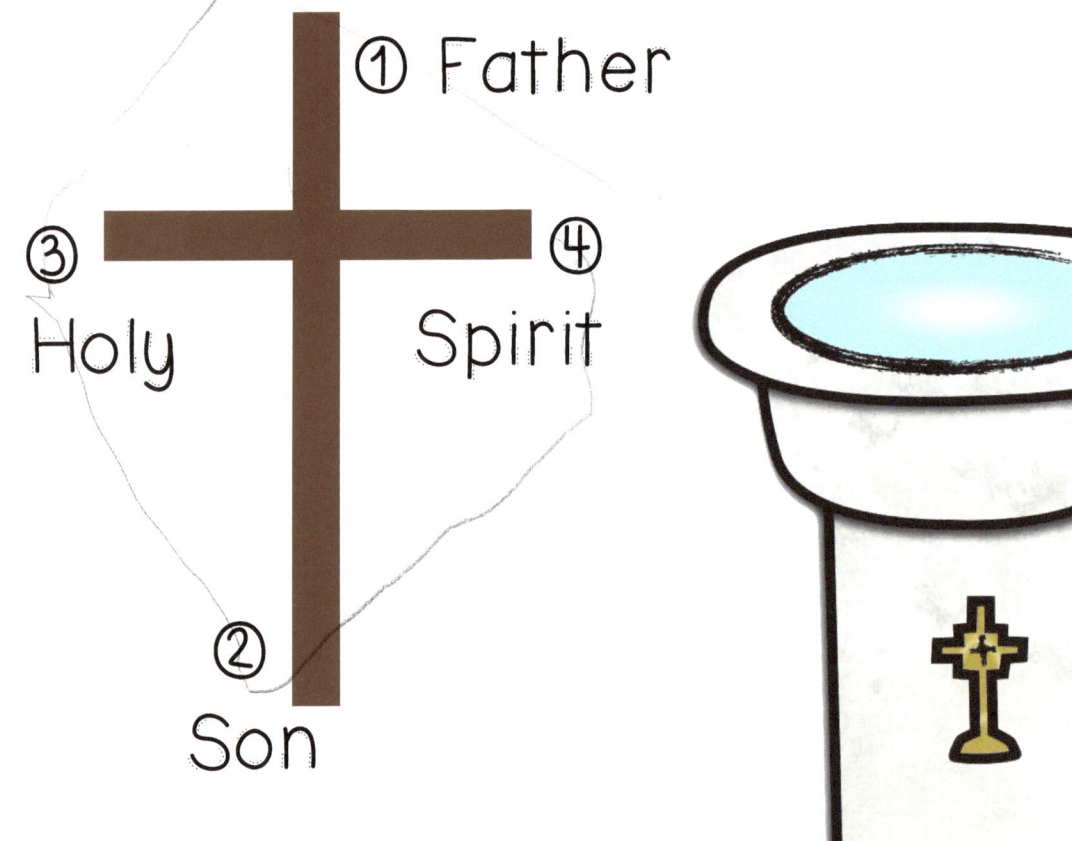

① Father
③ Holy
④ Spirit
② Son

In the name of the Father,
and of the Son,
and of the Holy Spirit.

What color are the priest's vestments?

Dress the priest. Store the other vestments on the correct color, OR simply trace your finger from the priest to the right colored vestment.

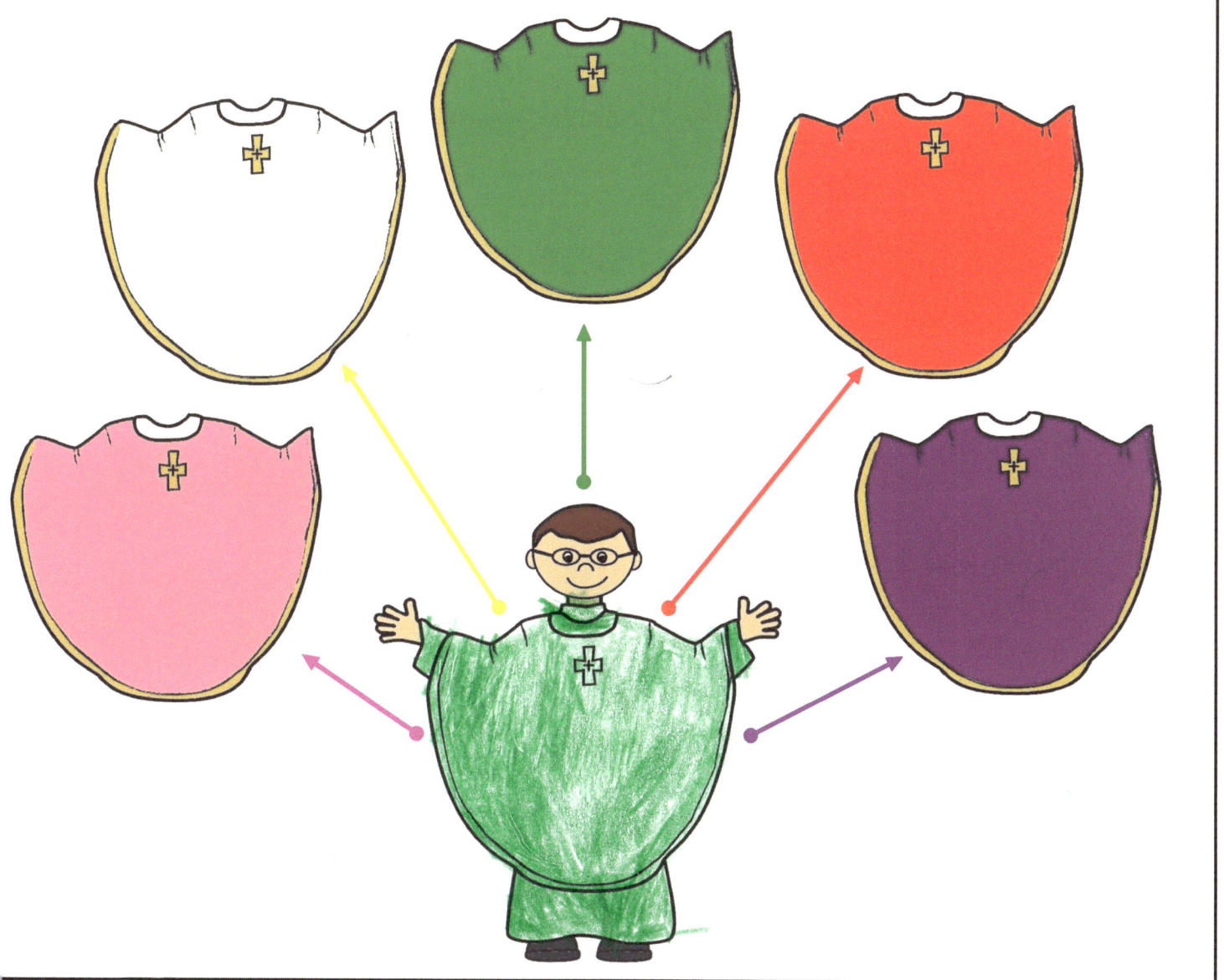

Confiteor

I confess to almighty God
and to you, my brothers and sisters,
that I have greatly sinned,
in my thoughts and in my words,
in what I have done and in what I have failed to do,

through my fault, through my fault,
through my most grievous fault;

therefore I ask blessed Mary ever-Virgin,
all the Angels and Saints,
and you, my brothers and sisters,
to pray for me to the Lord our God.

Kyrie

Lord, have mercy.
Christ, have mercy.
Lord, have mercy.

Or:

Kyrie, eleison.
Christe, eleison.
Kyrie, eleison.

Gloria

Glory to God in the highest,
and on earth peace to the people of good will.

We praise you,
we bless you,
we adore you,
we glorify you,
we give you thanks for your great glory,
Lord God, heavenly King,
O God, almighty Father.

Lord Jesus Christ, Only Begotten Son,
Lord God, Lamb of God, Son of the Father,

Gloria

you take away the sins of the world,

    have mercy on us;

you take away the sins of the world,

    receive our prayer;

you are seated at the right hand of the Father,

    have mercy on us.

For you alone are the Holy One,
you alone are the Lord,
you alone are the Most High,
Jesus Christ,
with the Holy Spirit,
in the glory of God the Father.
Amen.

Readings

Store your response cards here. Stick each one on the next page as you say the response OR slide your finger from the picture to the words as you say the responses.

Thanks be to God.

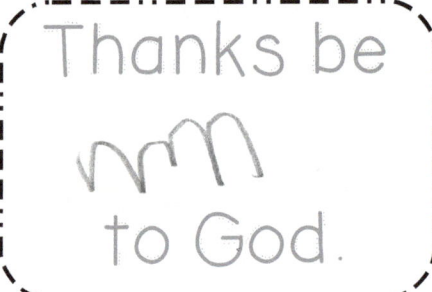

Thanks be to God.

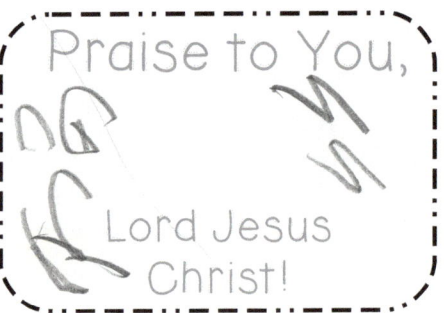

Praise to You, Lord Jesus Christ!

Readings

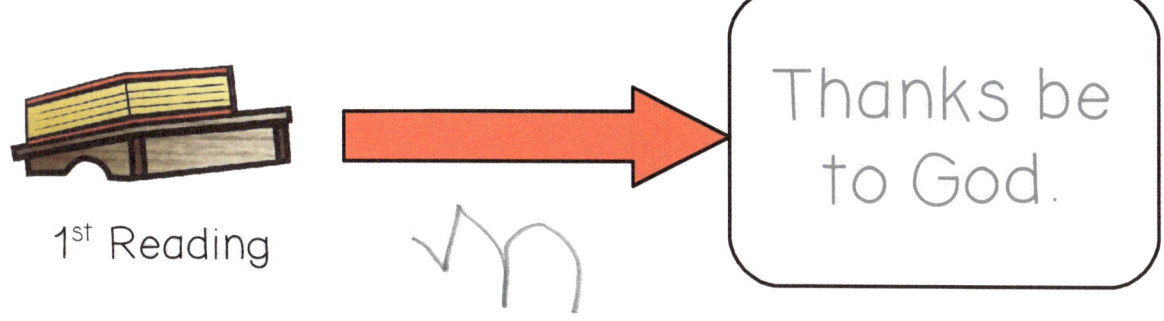

1st Reading → Thanks be to God.

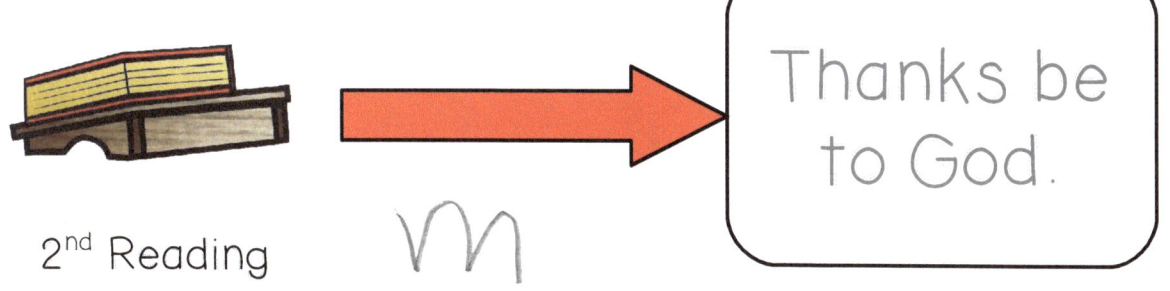

2nd Reading → Thanks be to God.

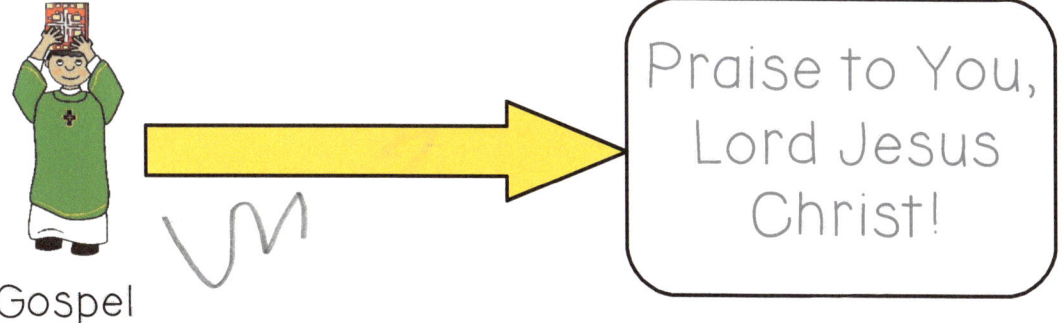

Gospel → Praise to You, Lord Jesus Christ!

What Can You Spot?

 Holy Water Font	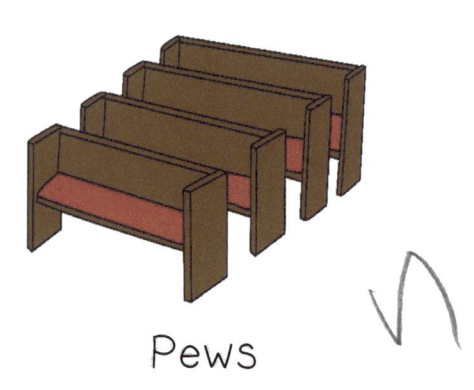 Pews	 Tabernacle
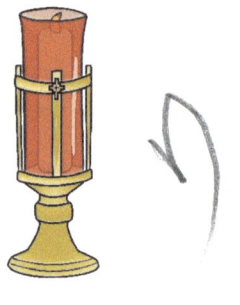 Sanctuary Candle	 Crucifix	 Roman Missal
 Ambo	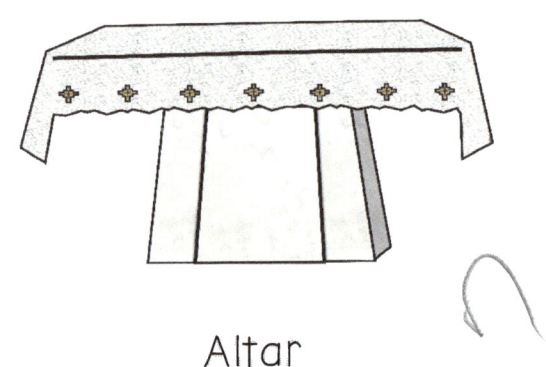 Altar	 Candle Taper

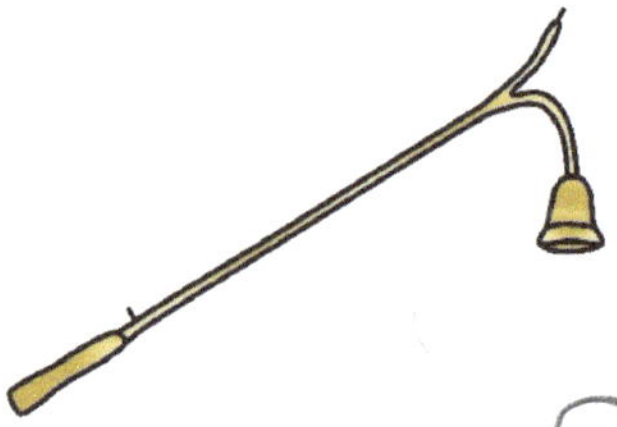

What Can You Spot?

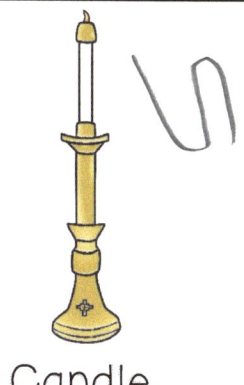 Candle	 Wine Pitcher	 Water Cruet
 Thurible	 Host	 Chalice
 Ciborium	 Purificator	 Bells

Profession of Faith

I believe in one God,
the Father almighty,
maker of heaven and earth,
of all things visible and invisible.

I believe in one Lord Jesus Christ,
the Only Begotten Son of God,
born of the Father before all ages.
God from God, Light from Light,
true God from true God,
begotten, not made, consubstantial with the Father;
through him all things were made.

For us men and for our salvation
he came down from heaven,
and by the Holy Spirit was incarnate of the Virgin Mary,
and became man.

Profession of Faith

For our sake he was crucified under Pontius Pilate,
he suffered death and was buried,
and rose again on the third day
in accordance with the Scriptures.
He ascended into heaven
and is seated at the right hand of the Father.
He will come again in glory
to judge the living and the dead
and his kingdom will have no end.

I believe in the Holy Spirit, the Lord, the giver of life, *white*
who proceeds from the Father and the Son,
who with the Father and the Son is adored and glorified,
who has spoken through the prophets.

I believe in one, holy, catholic and apostolic Church.
I confess one Baptism for the forgiveness of sins
and I look forward to the resurrection of the dead
and the life of the world to come. Amen.

Holy, Holy, Holy

Holy, Holy, Holy Lord God of hosts.

Heaven and earth are full of your glory.

Hosanna in the highest.

Blessed is he who comes in the name of the Lord.

Hosanna in the highest.

Our Father

Our Father, who art in heaven,
hallowed be thy name;
thy kingdom come,
thy will be done
on earth as it is in heaven.
Give us this day our daily bread,
and forgive us our trespasses,
as we forgive those who
trespass against us;
and lead us not into temptation,
but deliver us from evil.

For the kingdom,
the power and the glory are yours
now and for ever.

The Sign of Peace

How many people did you offer the Sign of Peace to today? Be sure to give a kind smile to each person!

"Peace be with you!"

Lamb of God

Lamb of God, you take away the sins of the world,
> **have mercy on us**.

Lamb of God, you take away the sins of the world,
> **have mercy on us**.

Lamb of God, you take away the sins of the world,
> **grant us peace**.

Holy Communion

Pay attention! Jesus has come to meet with you now. Have faith that he is really here – Body, Blood, Soul, and Divinity.

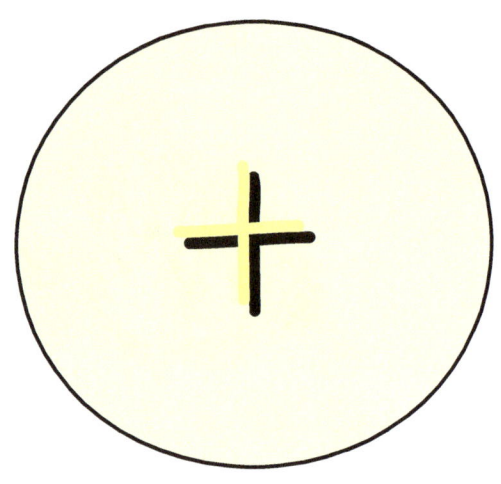

This is my body...

This is the chalice of my blood...

"Behold, the Lamb of God, who takes away the sin of the world!"
John 1:29

GO Forth!

Mass is almost over now. The priest blesses us with the Sign of the Cross. Thank Jesus for coming to visit with you today. This week, remember to share his love with everyone you meet!

I Pray After Mass

Thank you, Jesus, for meeting me at Mass today.

Mass is such a special time for me.

I know how much you love me.

Help me to love you back by being kind and loving to everyone I meet.

Amen.

Helpful Tips

If you are looking for the full instructions, please turn the page!

This page will give you some helpful tips on using the book.

①. Please know that if you can't or don't want to use the removable components in this book, it will still serve as a really nice book for your child. It is also okay to take the removable components away for a while if you find they aren't working for you. As they grow, you can always re-introduce them.

②. Don't stress if your child doesn't use the book in the way you anticipated. They may follow along perfectly, or they may flip back and forth to their favorite pages at will. Both are perfectly OK!

③. Before the first use, take 10-15 minutes to sit with your child and go over the pages. Have your child point out their favorite images and try the activities. This way, it isn't totally new the first time you head to Mass with it, because that can be distracting.

④. The first few times you use the book, your child may struggle to keep up or find their place. Try waiting to bring the book out until the homily, when they can spend a little uninterrupted time with it. Bring it out a little earlier at each Mass that you go to, and in this way you can help them learn to use it little by little.

⑤. You will notice that there are not many pages devoted to Holy Communion or to the Consecration. This is intentional on my part. Ideally children would set the book aside for the Consecration and turn their focus to Jesus. Eventually children should learn to turn inward in prayer during the reception of Holy Communion, but if they aren't ready for that, that is okay too.

⑥. The bottom line is that you should let your child use the book in the way that makes the most sense to them, and in the way that most helps them connect to what's happening at Mass.

Instructions

①. On the following pages you will find removable components to make your book more interactive for your child. Use scissors to cut the pages out of the book along the dotted line located on the left side of the page. Then cut out the vestments and response cards.

②. Laminate all the pieces that you have just cut out. You can use clear contact paper, making sure to cover both sides of the pieces (my favorite way), a home laminator, or you can take the pieces to your local teacher supply store and have them laminated very inexpensively. You really do need to laminate them somehow if you plan to use them long term.

③. I recommend using **Scotch Restickable Mini-Tabs for Mounting** (aka **Scotch Create Reusable Mini Squares**) to attach the vestments and cards to the correct pictures. They are available at Walmart or on Amazon. They look like small, clear squares that are sticky on both sides. The best way to attach the removable pieces is to place the sticky tab onto the back of each vestment or response card. Then line up the vestment or response card cut-out with its place in the book and press firmly. Super easy, and you can let your child help. Please note that the sticky tabs may lift a small amount of ink from the vestments the first few times you remove them. This should be viewed as normal wear and tear for this type of book.

④. Store the laminated cards on the correct pages in the interior of the book, and help your child place them in the correct spaces during Mass.

⑤. In the beginning, you should teach very young children to put the interactive components on firmly, and to pull them off gently. However, they will learn very quickly how much force to use for the best result. You can change out the tabs every few months with fresh ones if you feel they are losing their ability to adhere to the book.

Bonus: There are extra vestments and response cards included, so if you lose one of the removable components at Mass, you can always cut out another one!

Vestments

Read the instruction page to learn what to do with these.

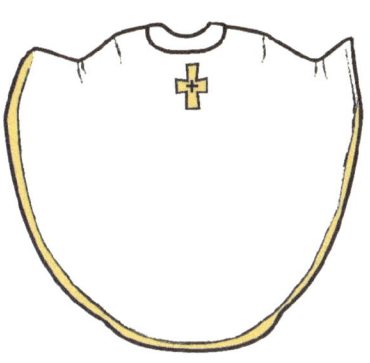

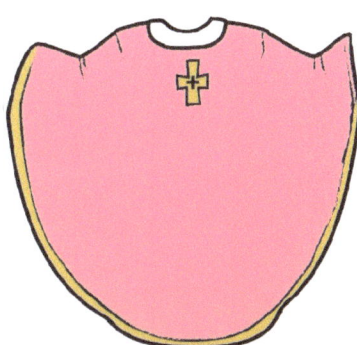

Readings

Read the instruction page to learn what to do with these.

> Thanks be to God.

> Thanks be to God.

> Praise to You, Lord Jesus Christ!

Vestments

If you happen to lose a vestment, here are some extras you can use.

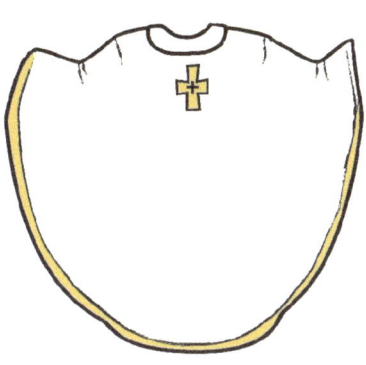

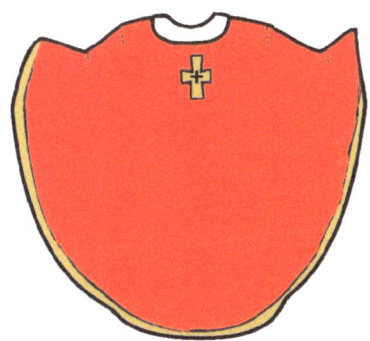
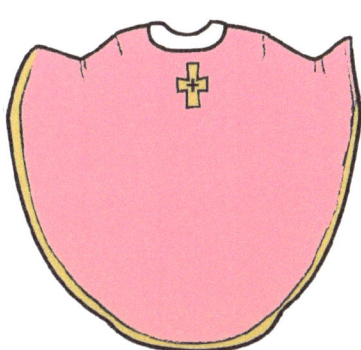

Readings

If you happen to lose a response card, here are some extras you can use.

Thanks be to God.

Thanks be to God.

Praise to You, Lord Jesus Christ!

CPSIA information can be obtained
at www.ICGtesting.com
Printed in the USA
BVHW02n0450141018
530046BV00001B/3/P